SURVIVOR

The Whaleship Essex
The True Story of Moby Dick

Jil Fine

HIGH
interest
books

Children's Press®
A Division of Scholastic Inc.
New York / Toronto / London / Auckland / Sydney
Mexico City / New Delhi / Hong Kong
Danbury, Connecticut

Book Design: Christopher Logan and Daniel Hosek
Contributing Editor: Matthew Pitt

Photo Credits: Front cover, Back cover, pp. 3, 11, 16, 21, © North
Wind Pictures Archive; pp. 4, 14, 24, 36 © Bettmann/Corbis;
pp. 5, 7, 9, 15, 25, 31, 37, 42, 43, 44, 45, 46, 47, 48 Dan Hosek;
p. 8 Library of Congress Maps Division; pp. 19, 32, 40 © Courtesy
of Nantucket Historical Association; p. 23 © Hulton/Archive/
Getty Images; p. 29 © Wolfgang Kaehler/Corbis

Library of Congress Cataloging-in-Publication Data

Fine, Jil.
  The Whaleship Essex : The True Story of Moby Dick / Jil Fine.
  p. cm. — (Survivor)
  Summary: Recounts the 1820 sinking of the whaleship "Essex" by
  an enraged sperm whale and how the crew of young men survived
  against impossible odds.
  ISBN 0-516-24328-4 (lib. bdg.) — ISBN 0-516-27872-X (pbk.)
  1. Essex (Whaleship)—Juvenile literature. 2. Shipwrecks—Pacific
  Ocean—Juvenile literature. [1. Essex (Whaleship) 2. Shipwrecks. 3.
  Whaling. 4. Survival.] I. Title. II. Series.

  G530.E77 F56 2003
  910'.9164'9—dc21

                                              2002153228

Contents

Introduction

The date is November 20, 1820. The shipmates of the whaleship *Essex* have been sailing the oceans for over 450 days, hunting one of nature's largest creatures—the mighty sperm whale. On this day, most of the crewmembers are out rowing smaller whaleboats. From these whaleboats, they will try to harpoon their giant prey. Suddenly, a massive whale is spotted. It disappears under the choppy waters. Moments later, a terrible jolt rocks the *Essex*. The whale has rammed the ship. The whale circles the boat and rams it again. Panicked, those men still on the *Essex* scramble onto a spare whaleboat. As the *Essex* sinks, so do the men's spirits. They realize they are stranded in the Pacific Ocean, and dry land is hundreds of miles away.

◀ When whalers took to the open seas, they found themselves battling one of Earth's most massive creatures: the sperm whale.

A year earlier, *Essex* had sailed from Nantucket Island, off the coast of Massachusetts. Nantucketers had been whaling for more than one hundred years. Never before had a whale attacked a ship. The story of the whaleship *Essex* stunned many people. The tale of those sailors who survived the attack shocked most people. It also inspired author Herman Melville to write his classic novel *Moby-Dick*. Read on to find out the true story behind his inspiration.

Voyage of the *Essex*
April 12, 1819—November 20, 1820

1 *Essex* launches from Nantucket Island
2 A storm knocks down *Essex*
3 *Essex* reaches the Azores island chain
4 *Essex* stops at the Cape Verde Islands
5 *Essex* successfully hunts whales in the winter and spring of 1820
6 *Essex* collects food on the Galapagos Islands
7 *Essex* is struck by sperm whale, November 20, 1820

North America

Europe

Africa

North
Atlantic Ocean

North
Pacific Ocean

Nantucket

Azores

Cape Verde
Islands

Atacames

South America

Galapagos
Islands

Offshore
Grounds

South
Pacific Ocean

South
Atlantic Ocean

60°N

60°N

15°S

30°S

45°S

60°S

75°S

105°W

90°W

45°W

30°W

15°W

In the eighteenth and early nineteenth centuries, Nantucket depended on whaling hunts to keep the town's businesses thriving.

One

Setting Sail

In the 1700s and 1800s, residents of the island of Nantucket were world famous for their whaling skills. Whalers would strip a dead whale's flesh and boil the blubber for oil. This oil could be used in many different items, such as lamps, candles, and lubricants. At first, Nantucketers killed right whales for oil. Right whales lived near the island's coast. By 1760, almost all of the right whales around Nantucket had been caught and killed.

Bigger, Faster, Better

Once their supply of right whales dwindled, Nantucketers started hunting sperm whales. Sperm whales live further out in the ocean than right whales. They are much swifter and more dangerous. Hunting sperm whales was worth the risk, however. Sperm whale oil burned cleaner and worked better than the oil from right whales. To hunt sperm whales, bigger ships were built. These ships had onboard ovens. Ovens let whalers boil the blubber into oil without having to return to land. Because of this, whaleships could stay at sea longer. Some sailed for two to three years at a time.

The Voyage Begins

On August 12, 1819, the *Essex* set sail. The ship's captain was twenty-eight-year-old George Pollard Jr. Though Pollard had sailed on the *Essex* for four years, this was his first trip in charge. Owen Chase was his first mate. Chase's job was to get the crew to perform Captain Pollard's orders. Many of these crewmembers were green hands. This meant they had no sailing experience. Chase shouted orders at the green hands as they worked to get the *Essex* out of the harbor. Cocky and ambitious, Chase was sure he had the same skills and talents as his captain— even though he was six years younger.

Since sperm whales lived so far offshore, whalers needed to stay at sea for months or years at a time. Having ovens onboard to boil blubber was a huge help to the whalers.

That night, Captain Pollard, first mate Chase, and second mate Matthew Joy each selected five men to crew the whaleboats. The whaleboats were attached to the sides of the *Essex*. The whaleboats would be lowered into the water once whales were spotted. Each whaleboat crew would try to harpoon and kill the whale. Two spare whaleboats were also onboard *Essex*.

Three crewmembers were to stay on the *Essex* while eighteen others were out in the whaleboats. These three men would be responsible for steering and handling the *Essex*.

Wicked Weather

On August 16, rain began to pour. Captain Pollard decided to leave some of the *Essex*'s sails up to test the ship's performance in stormy weather. Once Pollard saw lightning, he gave an order to shorten, or lower, the sails. His order came too late. The storm's strong winds slammed against the *Essex*. One side of the ship went completely underwater. The men held on to the rail for dear life. Time seemed to be at a standstill. Yet, ever so slowly, the *Essex* straightened, or righted, itself.

The storm had taken its toll. Several sails were ripped. The cookhouse, where the men's food was prepared, was destroyed. Two whaleboats had been lost and another was badly damaged. With only three whaleboats left, the men had no spares. Pollard wanted to return to Nantucket for repairs. Chase and Joy wanted to continue. They reminded Pollard that they would soon be stopping for supplies in the Azores, an island group near Portugal. There, they would probably find a spare whaleboat to buy. Was Pollard convinced by this argument? Was he uncertain of his own ability to lead? Whatever the reason, he soon gave in and gave the order to sail on.

Did You Know?

Right whales moved slowly, lived close to shore, and continued to float once they were killed. Because of this, whalers considered them the best, or right, whales to kill. This is how they got their name.

The Whale

In early September, the *Essex* reached the Azores. Unfortunately, the crew couldn't locate any spare whaleboats. The *Essex* sailed on to the Cape Verde islands. Another whaleship had wrecked there, and Captain Pollard was able to buy one of its whaleboats. Plus, Pollard was able to buy thirty live hogs for food.

The crew also had a good laugh at Cape Verde. As some of the crew steered a whaleboat into shore, it capsized. Several men, including Captain Pollard, tumbled head over heels into the water.

There She Blows!

The voyage's good fortunes continued into the fall. One day, the crewmember serving as lookout suddenly yelled, "There she blows!" Those words

On a whaleship, one crewmember always served as lookout. His job was to alert the crew the moment he spotted a whale in the water.

▲ Stripping blubber off the huge sperm whales was no small task for the *Essex*'s crew.

were music to whalers' ears. It meant a sperm whale had been spotted. Quickly the crew launched their whaleboats, rowing to the spot of the sighting. Chase's whaleboat was first to reach the whale. The boatsteerer stood at the front of the whaleboat, with harpoon in hand. Once harpooned, the whale swam off in pain and shock.

Since the harpoon was tied to the boat, the whale would drag the whaleboat along with it. Eventually, the whale grew tired of dragging all that weight. The men pulled closer. Then the mate stabbed the whale repeatedly with a 12-foot (3.7-meters) lance. The men slowly towed the whale's massive body back to the ship after it died.

A Trying Time

Once the men returned to *Essex*, they began the process of making whale oil, called trying-out. They tied the whale to the side of the *Essex*, cutting and ripping strips of blubber from its body. The blubber was put into huge pots. It took three days to boil the blubber into oil.

After the blubber was stripped, the crew cut the whale's head off. A sperm whale's head is filled with hundreds of gallons of spermaceti, which is very valuable oil. Using buckets, whalers were expected to scoop out every drop of spermaceti.

Going Offshore

Spring 1820 was good to the crew. They killed more than a whale a week. At the end of May, the *Essex* met up with another ship from Nantucket, the *Aurora*. The *Aurora* delivered letters from home to the *Essex*'s crew. The *Aurora*'s captain also advised Pollard about a new whaling spot. It was called the Offshore Grounds and was located in the North Pacific Ocean.

Pollard decided to head that way. To gear up for their travels, the *Essex* stopped for supplies in Atacames, a town in Ecuador. Once they reached town, sailor Henry DeWitt deserted, or left his job, on the *Essex*. Whaleships often had deserters. DeWitt's departure, though, would leave the *Essex* shorthanded. DeWitt was one of the three men who stayed with *Essex* while the whaleboats hunted. Now only two men would be left to care for the ship.

Since cabin boy Thomas Nickerson was steering *Essex* at the time it was attacked, he had the best view of the collision. This is a sketch he made of the whale's attack.

The *Essex* set sail for its final stop, the Galapagos Islands. There, the men caught 180 tortoises for food. On October 23, *Essex* set off for the Offshore Grounds.

The Real Moby Dick

On the morning of November 20, the three whaleboats sped to where several whales had been spotted. Chase's boat got extremely close to one. When a harpoon was plunged into its body, the whale smacked its tail against the boat.

Essex as she appeared on the morning of Nov 20th at

The force of the blow made a hole in the side of the whaleboat. While scrambling back to the *Essex*, the crew plugged this hole with their clothes. Chase furiously nailed a piece of canvas over the hole.

Meanwhile, Thomas Nickerson, a fifteen-year-old cabin boy, steered the *Essex* toward Pollard and Joy's boats. Both of them had successfully harpooned whales. As Nickerson drew the *Essex* near, he fixed his eyes on the largest whale he'd ever seen. It was about 85 feet (26 m) long. The whale dove, coming up about 35 yards (32 m) from the *Essex*. Waving its tail up and down, the whale charged the ship. Chase cried out for Nickerson to steer away, but it was too late. The whale rammed the front of the *Essex*. The force of the impact stunned the whale. As the woozy whale was recovering, Chase had a chance to kill it with a lance—but decided not to. Its giant tail was too close to the *Essex*'s rudder. If the tail smacked and destroyed the rudder, the men would not be able to steer the *Essex* back to land.

The furious lashings of a whale's tail posed huge problems for the hunting sailors.

Chase soon regretted his decision. At first, the whale began to swim away from the battered ship. Suddenly, the whale turned back around. It wasn't through with the *Essex*. The furious whale was now moving twice as fast as it had for its first attack. The whale struck the *Essex* a second time. It shoved the 238 ton (241.8 metric tons) ship backward with its tail as if it were a toy boat. Water poured into the whaleship. The whale finally swam off, but the damage had been done—*Essex* was sinking. The men lowered the

Did You Know?

Sperm whales communicate by making clicking sounds. Chase made similar sounds with his hammer while trying to nail the piece of canvas to his damaged whaleboat. The sounds may have attracted the whale's interest to the Essex.

spare whaleboat into the ocean. Steward William Bond dove into the captain's cabin to get Pollard and Chase's trunks and other equipment.

Meanwhile, the men in Pollard and Joy's boats had been busy trying to catch their whales. Obed Hendricks, a boatsteerer on Pollard's boat,

Because of the damage caused by the mighty whale, the *Essex*'s crew had no choice but to abandon ship.

glanced over his shoulder to see the *Essex* struggling to stay afloat. Pollard and Joy rowed to the wreck. They could not believe their ears when they were told of the whale's attack. As the *Essex* began to sink, her twenty-man crew began to wonder when—or if—they'd ever see land again.

Three

Stranded in the Pacific

Chase felt very guilty. He knew he should have lanced the whale when he had the chance. However, he and the others knew something far more important: They had little time to waste before the ship sank completely. Quickly, they collected 600 pounds (272 kilograms) of hardtack from the wrecked *Essex*. Hardtack is hard bread made from flour and water that must be soaked before it is eaten. The crew also gathered six Galapagos tortoises for food and enough fresh water for two months. William Bond's rescue dive provided Pollard and Chase each with a navigational book, a compass, and a quadrant, an instrument used to find a boat's latitude. Joy, however, would have no navigational equipment.

While the whale that attacked *Essex* didn't kill the crew, its attack put the men in serious peril. This illustration appeared in one printing of Herman Melville's *Moby-Dick*.

Preparing for the Worst

The crew took parts of the *Essex* to help strengthen the whaleboats. Men used the *Essex*'s sails to build sails for the whaleboats. They built up the sides of the whaleboats with wood from the *Essex*. Pollard decided it would be best to head for the Society Islands, which were 2,000 miles (over 3,000 kilometers) away. He believed they could reach the islands in about thirty days. Chase and Joy disagreed. The men knew little about the Society Islands. Chase and Joy worried that the islands' residents might be cannibals.

Did You Know?

To function properly, the human body needs at least 1 pint (0.47 liters) of water a day.

They proposed sailing for South America. Though this trip would take nearly twice as long, there was a greater chance that another whaleship would spot them. Again, Pollard backed down, and went along with Chase and Joy's plan.

Little Food, Less Water

The twenty men separated into three whaleboats. Pollard and Joy's boats each had seven men. Chase took only six men because his boat was the most damaged. In an attempt to stretch the food and water for the sixty-day journey, each man would get just 6 ounces (170 grams) of hardtack and a half pint (0.24 liters) of water a day.

On November 22, 1820, the whaleboats left the wreck of the *Essex* behind. After a few weeks, the men began to suffer from dehydration. Some men tried holding saltwater in their mouths to get moisture, but it only made them thirstier.

Unfortunately, the area where the men were sailing had very little marine life. The only food the area provided were flying fish and barnacles that grew on the bottoms of the boats. Chase was forced to cut his men's hardtack rations.

The Wrong Island

One month after the *Essex* sunk, the men had lost much of their strength. They were even losing some of their hair. The morning of December 20 began without fanfare. Nickerson remembered that his shipmates were "quite silent and dejected." Suddenly, around 7:00 A.M., nineteen-year-old sailor William Wright stood up and cried, "There is land!"

The men at first feared Wright was seeing a mirage. Soon, though, his vision was confirmed by every pair of eyes. Instantly, the men felt hopeful. Pollard and Chase decided that the island must be Ducie Island. Actually, it was Henderson Island, about 70 miles (112.7 km) west of Ducie Island.

The crew of the *Essex* took six Galapagos tortoises from the ship before it sank. While these animals provided nourishment for a while, the men soon found themselves starving again.

The boats landed and the men immediately got to work. They searched the island for fresh spring water and food. When Chase speared a fish, he and two other men ate it whole, including its scales and bones.

In the week that followed, the men caught all the food they could eat. Soon, the island's supply of crabs and fish became scarce. By December 26,

the men decided to leave. They would sail next to Easter Island, less than 1,000 miles (1.609.3 km) away.

Seth Weeks, William Wright, and Thomas Chappel informed the others that they would remain behind on the island. They believed the island offered a better chance of survival. Chappel, who was Matthew Joy's boatsteerer, had a second reason for staying. He could see that Matthew Joy's health was rapidly fading. If Joy died, Chappel would be forced to take command of Joy's whaleboat.

The Death of Joy

The next day, the three whaleboats—now carrying seventeen men—set sail once again. Their voyage was brutal. Strong winds pushed them far south of their destination. Within a week, they had given up trying to reach Easter Island. Pollard and Chase decided to try for a group of islands off the coast of Chile. However, they still had another 2,500 miles (over 4,000 km) to sail.

On January 10, 1821, Matthew Joy became the first crewmember to die. The men wrapped

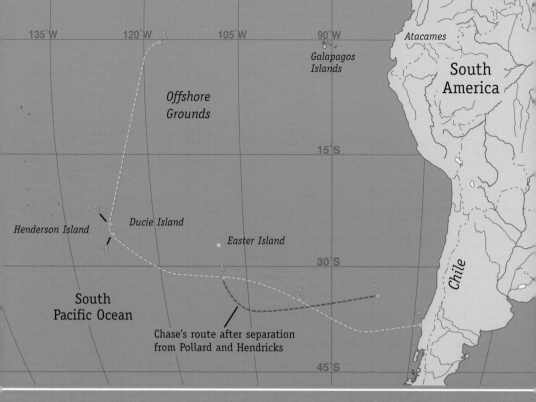

135°W   120°W   105°W   90°W   Atacames

Galapagos
Islands

South
America

Offshore
Grounds

15°S

2

Henderson Island   Ducie Island

Easter Island

3

30°S

Chile

South
Pacific Ocean

5   6

Chase's route after separation
from Pollard and Hendricks

7

45°S

▲ Voyage of the Whaleboats
November 20, 1820—February 18, 1821

1 *Essex* is struck by a sperm whale
2 The crewmembers spot Henderson Island
3 The crew departs from Henderson Island
4 Chase's whaleboat separates from the
   other two
5 The whaleboats of Pollard and Hendricks
   separate; Hendricks's boat and crew are
   never found
6 Chase's whaleboat is spotted and rescued,
   February 18, 1821
7 Pollard's whaleboat is spotted and rescued,
   February 23, 1821

him in clothes, tied a stone to his feet, and threw him overboard. Pollard sent his boatsteerer, Obed Hendricks, to lead Joy's boat.

The next day, a severe storm struck. Fierce wind and rain made it impossible for the whaleboats to spot one another. By the next morning, Chase's boat was separated from the other two. Neither Hendricks nor Pollard's crew could see any sign of Chase and his men.

Hendricks's boat wasn't faring much better. He and his crew had completely run out of food and water. Pollard's crew was running dangerously low as well. Nevertheless, they shared their

Twine made by Benjamin Lawrence while in the Boat. They were in the Boat 93 Days when the Ship Essex was shipwrecked. November 1819

small amount with their starving shipmates on Hendricks's whaleboat.

The death toll continued to rise. On January 20, one of Hendricks's crewmembers, Lawson Thomas, died. Hendricks, Pollard, and their crews were forced to make an extreme choice—to eat their fallen shipmate. They roasted pieces of Thomas's flesh, then ate them. Within another week, three more men died and were eaten. Those men were Charles Shorter and Isaiah Sheppard from Hendricks's boat, and Samuel Reed from Pollard's boat.

Somewhere during the unusually dark night of January 29, Hendricks's boat disappeared from Pollard's view. Obed Hendricks, William Bond, and Joseph West were never seen or heard from again.

Driven to Desperation

Meanwhile, Owen Chase's boat was having problems of its own. Chase was forced to cut his men's rations to a half ounce (14 g) of

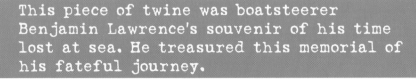

This piece of twine was boatsteerer Benjamin Lawrence's souvenir of his time lost at sea. He treasured this memorial of his fateful journey.

hardtack a day—a mere 2 tablespoons of bread! The men grew weaker by the day. Chase tried to stab a shark that swam near his boat. However, he was too weak to sink his knife into the shark's skin.

Starvation was taking its toll. On January 20, Richard Peterson refused his hardtack ration. "It may be of service to someone," said Peterson, "but can be of none to me." By late afternoon, Peterson's dehydration and starvation claimed his life. On February 8, Isaac Cole died. The next morning, Chase voiced what his crew was already thinking: that they eat Cole so that they would not be forced to kill one another. Cole's body provided food for Chase, Benjamin Lawrence, and Thomas Nickerson for three days.

Rescued!

On February 18, in Chase's whaleboat, Benjamin Lawrence saw a glimmer of hope in the distance. It was a sail! Chase, Lawrence, and Nickerson rowed their boat as fast as their tired bodies allowed. For the next three hours, the men raced toward the ship. Finally, someone onboard the ship—called the *Indian*—spotted the little whaleboat. When Chase and his men pulled up alongside the *Indian*, a ship's officer asked who they were. Chase barely had the strength to tell his tale. Once he did, the *Indian*'s captain, William Crozier, was moved to tears. Eighty-nine days after the *Essex* sunk, Chase, Lawrence, and Nickerson had been saved.

Elsewhere, Pollard's crew continued to dwindle. By February 11, both Owen Coffin and Barzillai Ray were dead. Now, from Joy and Pollard's whaleboats, only Pollard and Ramsdell remained. The two men were so weak they could barely stay conscious. Suddenly, on February 23, the silence of their ocean graveyard was broken by men's voices. The crew of the whaleship *Dauphin* had spotted the little whaleboat. When they peered into the whaleboat, they saw two men close to death, surrounded by a pile of human bones. The men of the *Dauphin* lifted Pollard and Ramsdell on their ship. They, too, had been saved.

Herman Melville's classic novel *Moby-Dick* was probably the most famous book to be based on the *Essex* whale hunt.

Four

The Survivors

Chase, Lawrence, and Nickerson were taken to Valparaiso, Chile. They arrived on February 25, 1821. Pollard and Ramsdell joined them on March 17. At first, Pollard made a quick recovery. He told his gripping, gruesome tale to several people, only to soon fall ill again. The other four whaleboat survivors left Chile on the *Eagle* to return to Nantucket on March 23. Pollard stayed behind. A trading vessel called the *Surry* volunteered to search for Chappel, Weeks, and Wright.

Life on Henderson Island

Chappel, Weeks, and Wright were still alive—on Henderson Island. They had survived on berries, shellfish, birds, eggs, and rainwater. You'll recall, however, that Pollard and Chase thought the island the crew landed on was Ducie Island!

When the *Surry* sailed by Ducie Island, their search came up empty. Luckily, the *Surry*'s captain guessed Pollard and Chase's mistake. On April 9, the *Surry* neared Henderson Island.

Meanwhile, Chappel, Weeks, and Wright were desperate. They ran their hands along caves, seeking drops of water for their dry lips. In the caves, they spotted a group of dead sailors from another expedition. The chilling sight made them wonder if they were next.

Finally, on April 9, their fortune changed. They spotted *Surry* attempting to come ashore. The waves were too rough for the ship to land. Terrified that the boat might leave, Chappel dove into the water, swam to the *Surry*, and was pulled aboard. The *Surry*'s crew thought they might have to return the next day to finish the rescue. Chappel refused to leave without his shipmates. Instead, he tied a rope around his waist and swam back to shore. With his last shred of strength, Chappel grabbed hold of

Weeks and Wright and the three men were towed to safety.

The Legend of the *Essex*

Of the twenty men on the *Essex* when it sank, only eight survived. The crew had been separated from their friends and families for nearly two years. Of course, they had expected to be gone this long, hunting whales. They never could have imagined, though, the horrors they would face in their time on the open seas.

When he returned to Nantucket on June 11, Owen Chase found he was a father. A fourteen-month-old daughter, Phebe Ann, was presented to him. Chase's wife, Peggy, met with an even greater shock: The husband she had believed dead was standing before her, though thin and wounded from his ordeal. Chase would later write a book about his experience. Thomas Nickerson also wrote about the *Essex*. He did not write his book until he was seventy-two, though. It wasn't published until 1984.

Herman Melville read Chase's book to get inspiration for his classic novel *Moby-Dick*. In Melville's novel, Captain Ahab leads the whaleship *Pequod* on a whale hunt. Ahab is a cruel captain who wants to destroy a giant, white sperm whale. Ahab pursues the powerful whale with furious anger.

The brave actions of the *Essex*'s crew have inspired and amazed people for nearly two hundred years. For their courage and their will to survive, the crew will long be remembered.

Owen Chase (left) and Thomas Nickerson (right) astounded readers with gripping accounts of their tragic adventure.

The crew of the whaleship *Essex* have been sailing the seas for over 450 days hunting for whales. During a hunt, they are rammed by a sperm whale in the North Pacific Ocean, off the coast of South America. The *Essex* sinks, leaving the twenty-man crew stranded on the high seas in three small whaleboats. For the next five months, the men do all they can to deal with hunger and thirst—and the continuing deaths of their shipmates. Only eight men survive their incredible journey.

- April 12, 1819 *Essex* launches from Nantucket Island
- Early September *Essex* reached the Azores chain
- Mid-September *Essex* stops at the Cape Verde Islands
- Late May, 1820 The *Essex* learns about the Offshore Grounds
- October *Essex* collects food on the Galapagos Islands
- October 23 *Essex* sets off for the Offshore Grounds
- November 20 *Essex* is struck by sperm whale
- November 22 The whaleboats sail away from the wrecked *Essex*
- Late December The whaleboats stop at Henderson Island; three crewmembers remain behind
- January 10, 1821 Matthew Joy is the first crewmember to die
- January 12 Chase's whaleboat separates from the other two
- January 20 Lawson Thomas dies and is eaten by the survivors
- January 20 Richard Peterson dies on Chase's whaleboat
- Late January Three more crewmembers die
- January 29 Hendricks's whaleboat separates from Pollard's; the boat and crew are never found
- February 8 Isaac Cole dies on Chase's whaleboat
- February 11 Two crewmembers die on Pollard's whaleboat
- February 18 Chase's whaleboat is rescued by the *Indian*
- February 23 Pollard's whaleboat is rescued by the *Dauphin*
- February 25 Chase, Lawrence, and Nickerson arrive in Chile
- March 17 Pollard and Ramsdell arrive in Chile
- April 9 *Surrey* rescues Chappel, Weeks, and Wright on Henderson Island

NEW WORDS

barnacles (**bar**-nuh-kuhlz) small shellfish that attach themselves firmly to the sides of boats, rocks, and other shellfish

blubber (**bluh**-bur) the fat under the skin of a whale or seal

boatsteerer (**boht**-stihr-uhr) the crewmember on a whaleboat that is in charge of harpooning the whale

cannibals (**kan**-uh-buhlz) people who eat human flesh

dehydrated (dee-**hye**-dray-tid) not having enough water in your body

harpoon (har-**poon**) a long spear with an attached rope that can be thrown; to hit or kill with a harpoon

lance (**lanss**) a long spear

latitude (**lat**-uh-tood) the position of a place, measured in degrees north or south of the equator

NEW WORDS

mirage (muh-**razh**) something a person thinks he or she sees in the distance that is not really there

Offshore Grounds (**off**-shor **groundz**) an area in the Pacific Ocean where whalers found many whales to hunt

quadrant (**kwahd**-ruhnt) an instrument used by sailors to find at what latitude their boats are positioned

ration (**rash**-uhn) a limited amount or share, especially of food

spermaceti (**spurm**-uh-seh-tee) a very valuable oil found in the large sac in a sperm whale's head

steward (**stoo**-urd) a man who serves passengers on a ship

trying-out (**trye**-ing-out) the process by which whale blubber is made into oil

whalers (**way**-lur) people who hunt whales

whaleship (**wale**-ship) a large ship that was used for hunting whales

FOR FURTHER READING

Carrick, Carol. *Whaling Days*. New York: Houghton Mifflin, 1993.

Melville, Herman. *Moby-Dick*. Mahwah, NJ: Troll Communications L.L.C., 1990.

Murphy, Jim. *Gone A-Whaling*. New York: Houghton Mifflin, 1998.

Papastavrou, Vassili. *Eyewitness: Whale*. New York: DK Publishing, 2000.

Philbrick, Nathaniel. *Revenge of the Whale: The True Story of the Whaleship "Essex."* New York: Penguin USA, 2002.

ORGANIZATIONS

International Fund for Animal Welfare

411 Main Street
P.O. Box 193
Yarmouth Port, MA 02675
(508) 744–2000
(800) 932–4329
www.ifaw.org

Nantucket Historical Association

P.O. Box 1016
Nantucket, MA 02554
(508) 228–1894
E-mail: nhainfo@nha.org
www.nha.org

New Bedford Whaling Museum

18 Johnny Cake Hill
New Bedford, MA 02740–6398
(508) 997–0046
Fax: (508) 997–0018
www.whalingmuseum.org

WEB SITES

MSNBC: Revenge of the Whale

www.msnbc.com/modules/tvnews/whalerevenge/
This Web site has pictures, maps, diagrams, and even audio features that will provide in-depth information on the whaleship *Essex*.

PBS: Voyage of the Odyssey: Whaleship *Essex*

www.pbs.org/odyssey/class/essex.html
This Web site has a lot of information about the *Essex* and sailing.

Wonders of the Sea: Sperm Whales

www.oceanicresearch.org/spermwhales.htm
Find out about sperm whales on this informative Web site.

INDEX

INDEX

ABOUT THE AUTHOR

Jil Fine is a writer and editor living in New York. She plans to sail in the Pacific Ocean one day and to avoid angry sperm whales.